Every Single Type Of Air

A collection

Courtney Kitts

BookLeaf Publishing

India | USA | UK

Made with ❤ on the BookLeaf Publishing Platform

www.bookleafpub.in

www.bookleafpub.com

Dedication

There are a million ways to absorb the world
And none of mine made sense
I hope someone feels the same words

Preface

I've never been a pill you could take without water.
I can only hope
The taste doesn't linger on your tongue.

Acknowledgements

To everyone that has listened to insane passionate
ramblings
Or songs
Or novels
Or poems.
Thank you for supporting even the projects that didn't
earn it.

1. Kaleido

Kaleido was a silly girl who viewed the world quite
strangely
She'd always speak in little rhymes, her mother'd sigh
"speak plainly"
And in her quiet little town, she couldn't find much hope
Because everything that people felt fit in Kaleido's scope.
Her mother thought in black and white. Her father only
numbers.
Kaleido never understood how not to understand others.
So when a man came into town who saw in blinking
lights
The people in her town were mad and ready for a fight.
They gathered in the square and yelled and tried to chase
him out
While Kaleido tried to meet the man who reminded her
of herself.
"Careful now, Kaleido" Mom scolded through her teeth
"We should be kind but can't be kind to everyone we
meet."
"Some people are just born wrong; they never stood a

chance.

They have a place, but it's not here. We shouldn't hold their hands."

But Kaleido saw him laughing, and listening to the breeze

And Kaleido was so jealous of how he laughed with all the trees.

Her parents always scolded her for playing in the rain

And her friend said "what a silly girl" when her tights were always stained.

Her teachers always reprimanded her for being loud

And the grownups whispered back and forth when she talked to the clouds.

But this stranger in the park one day was singing to a bird

And Kaleido looked around and saw that no one else had heard

And she saw the bird the way he did and saw everyone else didn't

And wondered if they'd change their minds if only they would listen.

She saw he saw things differently and finally understood

That no one tried to see like him, she really wished they would.

But for the first time in her young life, she felt a little hope

Because everyone Kaliedo met fit in Kaliedo's scope

2. The Sounds & The Silence

I couldn't squeeze my eyes closed any tighter.

I heard the expansion.

I heard the compression.

I heard it over and over again

until my own breathing synced up.

My head was burried in my husband's chest.

I know the room was full

But I tried as hard as I could to pick my mother's breath

out of the crowd.

Then my Oma's.

All I could find was my husband's

Which makes sense because I was using his lungs as

earmuffs.

I heard the nurses speak.

I heard the pastor pray.

I tried to block it out.

To focus on the in and out.

The up and the down.

The mechanics that I could make sense of.

I heard it stop.

I heard the "Amen."
I heard the gasp.
I heard the rattle.
I heard the nurse explain.
I didn't move.
I kept my face burried.
I tried to find the breathing that I couldn't ignore before.
It was all just ringing and echoes.
Then it got blurry.

I left the room.
I went somewhere on my own.
I tried to find somewhere quiet.
No where was but my feet just kept pulling me with
them.
I listened to alarms
And codes
And crying
Until I didn't know where I was.
Until I was on the phone and wasn't sure how I got
there.
But then I heard my aunt in tears.
So I dried my eyes
And focused on my breathing
And tried to find my way back to where I was
Before the breathing stopped.

3. Honey Suckle & Ivy

I couldn't find that creek again if I spent my whole life
looking.
I wonder if you remember how to find the path.
I wonder if the water is as deep as I remember.
I wonder if the tree at the split in the water is still
protected
by the castle walls we built around the roots
with the biggest rocks our toothpick arms could carry.
I wonder if they'd feel heavy at all now.

I can hardly recognize those little girls
catching salamanders
and throwing mud.
Now I hate to get my hair wet.
Your day is ruined when you scuff your sneakers.

The last time I saw you was at a funeral.
You called my boyfriend by my ex husband's name.
I asked how you were liking Texas.
You said you moved back 6 years ago.

We hugged and said we would catch up soon
and shuffled off to find our mothers in the pews.

We never did catch up.
You have a life
And I have mine
And we don't still have that book we took turns keeping,
Writing daily letters so the next time we saw each other
we were sure we wouldn't forget any stories.

My hair is curlier now.
You grew out your bangs.
If we bumped into each other in public
I'm not sure we would even notice anymore.

But today I smelled a candle
That smelled like honey suckle and ivy
And I swear I could hear you crawling through the
leaves behind me
At that creek;
Laughing and trying to scare your little brother
With the frogs we had cupped in our hands.
When I put the candle down, I remembered our mothers
With disapproving looks on their faces
Setting down their coffee cups
And going to run us a bath.

I almost called you
but I didn't.
I did buy the candle.

4. Emergency Room

It's funny how caught people get in their own moment.
Their own lives.
It's thanksgiving and everyone else in the city is
gathering
And remembering
And celebrating.
Everyone in this room is scared and suffering.
We have more in common right now than any other
room in this town
But the isolation here is not lost on me.
Everyone is quiet.

I'm sitting alone with an IV and a wheelchair
Trying to do the math on the seconds I can keep looking
at friend's photos
Compared to the battery life left on my phone.
I can't help but look around.

A woman is sleeping in the corner.
A husband looks terrified while his wife smiles, holds his

hand,
And tries not to show the pain in her throat.
A man in the back keeps ducking down in his chair
Hoping no one sees him.
He seems to not have another warm place to go.
He pretends to be asleep when the nurse passes,
Silently hoping for another five minutes of no one
deciding he shouldn't be here.
In the middle of the room is a family.
I know one of the girls my age from work but not well
enough to address it.
I try not to make eye contact because she has enough
going on.
They are all crying and praying in a language I don't
understand
Over a man that seems unstartled and unbothered
But I am not oblivious to the fact that every time he
turns to cough
He whimpers softly and holds his stomach
And hopes the kids don't see.
The nurses are calling names as fast as they can.
The people in the chairs don't think it's fast enough.
I wonder if anyone else has looked around the room.

A woman yells at the receptionist.
The security guard checks for badges
So I wheel over to the man slinking in his chair

And loudly thank him for coming to make sure I'm not
scared.
Security keeps walking.
I put $5 in the vending machine before I "remember" I
am not allowed to eat
And wheel away.
The man thanks me.
I try to fake confusion.

The family keeps praying.
I look at the nurses and try to wonder what they are
going home to after this.
I see the stress in their forced smiles
And wonder if someone will offer them a blanket to
relax
Like they offered me.
I hope they do.

I can taste the air in the room.
It is salty, and scared, and isolating.
I wonder if I am the first person to experience
This combination of flavors.
I look around and am sure I am not.
Somehow, I'm sure I'm the only one who knows this.

So I don't stare when the woman throws her orange juice
at another patient.

Everyone laughs when security removes her
Before returning to their own moment
Alone
Or with their partner
Or with their whole family.
I don't laugh.
Instead, I wonder where she is going after this.
I wonder what that wait time is at that hospital.
I hope it's shorter
Because I heard her crying with each sip of water.

Everyone is in their own world
But everyone is suffering.
Families are breaking wishing bones,
And recalling successes,
Or even planning the night's big buys.
In here it is still
And hard
And cold
And we all feel it.
So I just quietly watch the hope fall in every face
When the name that gets called next isn't theirs.
I wonder if they think the woman calling the names
doesn't see.

5. Thank You

I am having a bad day.

I woke up with a bloody nose that I am fairly sure I

somehow broke

In my sleep.

Yet again

Because the night terrors have been getting the best of

me.

I walked out onto my balcony and the construction crew

was there

Again

Which is no surprise because the new building is already

a year past projections.

One of the guys yelled something at me

But I recognized the tone of voice and didn't look up

from my phone.

I don't like to be a rude person

But at a certain point

You just can't hear "Come on over, baby girl"

One more time

Before you've had a chance to drink your coffee.

My stomach really hurts today
But I guess it does most days.
It's been really bad lately
But today isn't ER bad
And I know everyone is tired of worrying
And I don't want to make it worse.
So it's fine.
I called a friend to cheer me up before I head in to work.
While I am walking to my car
A man from the construction crew catcalled me
Across the parking lot
For a straight minute.
I swore into my phone
And tried not to make eye contact.
I got the bread the bar needed from the store.
One man hit my ankle with a cart and then called me
sweetheart.
One man heard me complain into my earbuds
That I was "really tired of guys today"
And told me he could change my mind.
One man heard me make a vague threat to "the next guy
who...."
Into my phone
And gave me a dirty look before turning down the aisle.
I told my friend I felt bad but maybe I should try that
approach more often.
But I went into work.

I ended my phone call and said I was sorry for being so
negative.
I've just been really struggling lately.
And work has been hard.
And people have been mean.
And my medical bills are adding up.
And I really just need a good night's sleep
And a day off work.
But I shouldn't be so negative.
And it's fine.
And I'm fine.

I turned off my car and carried the bread into work.
I smiled and apologized that it took so long.
The bartender cut me off and asked if I had ordered
ketchup.
The line cook rolled his eyes and said it was the wrong
brand.
A guest yelled out for napkins.
So I got them a napkin
And I asked if anyone needed anything before I went to
my office
and tried not to calculate how many days it has been
Since anyone has said thank you.

6. Faith

My mother always told me to pray every night.
To give myself completely.
To put in all the faith I had.
And I did.
But one day I started to lose it.

Then I found you
And every night I closed my eyes and told you I loved
you
And I needed you to stay
And it was the simplest
Purest
Prayer.
And I put all my faith in you
And damn
Did I worship you.

But one day I started to lose you.

Now I guess I've lost my faith.

7. Natural Disasters

My Oma always told me there were two types of people
And for a very long time, I believed her.
There were tornadoes
Who trash around
Blindly,
Hoping to catch someone
And consume all that they are
In the most passionate,
Spontaneous way.
Whereas others are like mountains
And simply wait for someone to try and climb them.

Now I know she was wrong.
Yes,
There are tornadoes and there are mountains
But no one warned me about rainstorms
That destroy you in passing
With no acknowledgement of what they have done.
Or the wildfires
That burn so fast and so bright

And then disappear with a cloud of smoke.
No one told me about the oceans
Who loyally return after each dismissal,
Fearless and optimistic
Of each new tide.
Or even the suns
Who let you take what you need
Even if it's from them
And then hide away until you need them again.

No one told me and no one seems to be able to see
And that's why love is so wrong and so broken.
Lover's spine alone thinking they are dancing
When they're really stuck in a hurricane
And people think they feel the sun
And never feel the flames.
And people are so blind to themselves that they never
even see the person
That they just burnt to the ground
Or left buried in an avalanche
Or climbing out of the crater
And everyone overlooks how even the ocean's loving
arms
Can drown you.

8. Poetry

I tried to write you a poem.
I scribbled your name at the top of the page
And then I had to stop
Because I realized it was perfect.

I still think it was my best writing.

9. Writer's Block

I've been trying to teach myself that pain isn't beautiful.

Art is hard to see through whiskey eyes
And a cigarette smoke screen.
I tried for so long to find something
Majestic
In this misery,
Some solace in this solitude,
But pain isn't beautiful.

I haven't felt much like poetry lately.

10. 409B

I can't drink enough whiskey
To make me forget the nights on your roof
Or the morning's in your living room.
I can't breathe in enough smoke
To cough you out of my lungs
For more than a few hours.
Every time I think you are gone
I find you
Tangled in my hair
Or wrapped between my fingers.
And you're never missing long enough to forget the way
you taste.

11. Fake ID

I never smoked like you did
But you had lips like nicotine
And since you left
I'll do anything for a fix.
You have whiskey eyes and if I look into them long
enough
I forget what exactly I had to say.

I liked you because you were the first man to ever make
me feel like and adult
But once you left
I realized I was just a little girl
Playing dress up in her mother's heels
And I have never felt more like a child.

My parents still ask about you.
These days I talk about you like a bedtime story.
Some days you are the prince
And others you are the evil wizard.
Even I don't know what is the truth.

I need you like a blanket
Or a nightlight
Or my old favorite teddy bear
But you are just a shot of tequila
And you only ever come at last call.

12. Morning Routine

Some days I can taste your lips first thing in the
morning.

I kick the blankets to make sure you're not still in there
Counting the days until I find you
The same way I have been counting the days since you
left.

I pour coffee,
Black.
I don't let it cool so I don't have to taste it.
Acid churns my stomach
The same way hearing your name still does.
I stick my tongue to the roof of my mouth.
I draw a long breath through my nose.
I close my eyes.
Anything to keep it down.

I grab a cigarette.
I don't cough anymore just to spite how you said it was

cute

But I still exhale the way you taught me.
I try not to think about what that means.

I skip breakfast.
I pull my dirty hair into a ponytail.
I still make sure I'm wearing my cutest undershirt
Just in case when I get home
You're there waiting
With a bagel and a story
About how you've been trying to your way back to me
all along.

13. Enigma

I swear you can tell when it's going to rain
And grab your hat before even blows.
One night I heard you counting the stars.
I don't understand how you do that.

I think you can trace patterns in the wind
And walk between rain drops to stay dry.
I'm almost sure I've heard you talk to the sea.
I don't understand how you do that.

Your smile can summon a sunrise
And one flutter of your eyelids calls the moon to the sky.
Your tears always bring on a hurricane.
I don't understand how you do that.

I think the world stops spinning when you sleep
And somedays move slower, just for you.
You walk on water like the damn messiah come again.
I don't understand how you do that.

14.

The sun casts tiny rainbows
Across the still surface of the lake.
Birds sing in the distance
As a soft white cloud drifts
Benevolently
Across the pale blue sky.
The water is still and serene.

Underneath it's surface,
I am sinking.

15. NASA

On my eighteenth birthday, I wrote you a poem
About the moon
And the stars
And the telescope on your roof.
That night you painted entire constellations into my
spine.
Ever since,
I've been afraid to look at the stars.

I remember wondering how a mouth like yours could
even use the word "love"
but I sucked in every molecule.
I once read that every breath you take
Kills three cells in your body.
I was sure breathing in that one word froze them all.

I kept that poem
Only now,
I wear it on my thigh like a tattoo
Along with every

"She meant nothing"
"I take it back!"
"I never signed up to be your doctor, damn it!"
But no matter how much you take it back,
You can't undo it.
No matter how much you try,
You can't change it.
Maybe that's why you never tried at all.

It's been years now
But someone at work today brought up a documentary
about a black hole.
They asked if I had seen it.
I paused for a second
Before I very simply stated
"I've never been that interested in outer space."

16. Vanna

I woke up last night to the sound of a girl crying.
Her words were so muffled
That I could barely make them out.
She whimpered when she couldn't speak
Like the silence hurt.
Through the phone,
I could see how red her face was.
I almost thought it was you.
It wasn't
And it never will be.
Because I almost stayed on the phone.
I almost didn't believe you when you said you would be
fine.
I almost tried hard enough.

So I stayed tonight
And I listened
And made her keep breathing
Even when she swore she didn't need it
Because I didn't when it mattered.

It was almost enough.

31

17. I Don't Have The Words

Nothing I can say
Can bring you back.
i won't try.

I miss you.

18. Endings

Three lines can't explain
How much I wish you miss me
Like you pretend to.